LOOK OUT FOR THE BULL!

LOOK OUT FOR THE BULL!

BY
BILL BULLINGTON

Look Out For The Bull!
Published through Lulu.com

All rights reserved
Copyright © 2005 by William Bullington

Book Design and Layout by
www.integrativeink.com

- The general information on investing presented in this book does not involve the rendering of personalized investment advice and is not a substitute for engaging the services of a qualified financial advisor. Information contained in this book is not an offer to buy or sell or a solicitation of any offer to buy or sell the securities mentioned herein.

- The information presented in this book is believed to be factual and current at the time of its publication. The author does not guarantee its accuracy and it should not be regarded as a complete analysis of any of the subjects discussed. All expressions of opinion reflect the judgment of the author as of the date of publication and are subject to change.

- All investment strategies have the potential for profit or loss. Past performance may not be indicative of future results.

TABLE OF CONTENTS

INTRODUCTION

I wrote this book with the beginning investor in mind.

On my radio program, and during many of the seminars I conduct, I'm often asked what books a beginner should read in order to learn how to invest in the stock market. I've always been at a loss for beginning investors because I've felt that most books on investing in stocks, even those that claim to be written for beginners, are not really written with the beginner in mind. Many who are new to studying the stock market may become confused and discouraged by the complexity of books on investing and end up giving up on them before they finish reading them. With that in mind, just how does a beginner with no formal education in accounting or finance learn the skills necessary to pick stocks?

This is where I come in. In addition to hosting a weekly radio program and regular monthly seminars, I also manage a hedge fund and private accounts for clients. My first goal in writing this book is to get you to the point where you will know the difference between a high-risk stock, which could cause you to lose a substantial portion of your money, and a low-risk stock with a potentially high return. The basic idea is that you'd like to find stocks that are undervalued for purchases, and then learn to identify stocks that are overvalued and due for a fall so that you can avoid them. That makes sense, doesn't it? Wanting to buy stocks that are undervalued and avoid those that are overpriced? By the way, that's the main difference between a professional investor and an amateur. An amateur thinks that to make large gains you've got to take large risks. A professional investor looks for a low risk opportunity with high return potential.

When you know how to evaluate a stock, both on the basis of risk involved and on potential return, you'll know how to investigate the hot tip from your broker, barber, or any other well-meaning tipster before you invest your hard-earned money. If you have access to the Internet, you should be able to complete the analysis in two minutes or less.

The second goal I have for this book is to make it easy to read. Sticking to that theme, this book is *not* filled with complicated formulas, and you will not need a background in accounting to understand how to evaluate a stock. What you will walk away with, hopefully, are the basics of sound stock selection. By understanding and executing the basics of sound investing (as with many other things in life), you should win more than you lose—and you might just make a lot of money.

Before we get started, let me tell you how the book is formatted. First and foremost, I am not of the opinion that bigger is necessarily better. I believe that you should make your point as quickly and as simply as possible, which should come as a great relief to people who know me personally and are familiar with my tendency to talk.

The book starts off with a worksheet that I use to estimate a stock's fair market value. The remainder of the book is split into sections. Each section will have two parts. The first part will begin with an explanation of how to make the calculations found on the worksheet and will be in ***bold, italic print***. The second part of the section will be a discussion on the reasons I've chosen to perform the calculations the way I have, along with an example.

I wrote the book this way because it's been my experience that if you give someone rules to follow without telling them why the rules work, then they will probably not follow them. In breaking down each section into a "how to" section and an "explanation and example" section, I'm trying to keep it easy to read. If you are an experienced investor, you can skip the discussion sections and finish this book in about 20 minutes. If you are like I was when I began, you can read the book in about an hour and then go back to specific sections when you begin to use the worksheet on your own.

In the final sections of the book, I'll provide you with some guidelines to running a complete stock portfolio using the material you've learned.

All of the information you will need to fill out the worksheet can be found in many ways, thanks to the Internet. You can go to the Securities and Exchange Commission's home page at www.sec.gov and look up the last five years of a company's financial statements as well as at least five years worth of data on a dozen or more companies in the same industry to perform all the necessary calculations. Be prepared to quit your day job if you take this route.

Value Line, a financial reporting service, carries all of the information you'll need on roughly 1,700 stocks and a couple hundred industry groups as well. I'm not here to sell Value Line, and they didn't sponsor this book; still, in my opinion, it's definitely worth the subscription price for the time it will save you.

If you don't want to pay for Value Line, you can go to www.moneycentral.com, owned by Microsoft. There are many other free financial web sites that you can use to gather the information you'll need, and there are new ones springing up all of the time. I mention the Microsoft web site because with the way the information on their web site is formatted, it's very easy to gather the data we need in a short time period. I will give you a warning, however. I have found that free financial web sites tend to change frequently. The information that is there now may not be there a month from now. Also, I've found some data that wasn't terribly accurate. It's fairly rare that inaccuracies show up, but they do happen from time to time. The tendency for errors to occur in financial publications is one of the many reasons we diversify our stock holdings. Call it information diversification if you wish. The last thing you want to do is invest heavily in a stock only to find out that the numbers upon which you based your estimate were wrong!

Having said that, no matter which service you decide to use, here are the key items you are looking for:

1. Sales or revenues over the last twelve months.

2. The percent sales are up or down over the last twelve months.

3. The company's average profit margin (if you are calculating this yourself, I'd look at the last five years, at least, as an average).

4. The industry's average profit margin.

5. The total number of shares the company has outstanding.

6. The Debt to Equity Ratio.

Once you have all of these pieces of information, you will be ready to perform the analysis, which should take you about 30 seconds with a calculator once you have some practice. (The other minute and a half of the two minutes I spoke of earlier is spent looking up the information.) Ready? Then let's get started.

ESTIMATED FAIR MARKET VALUE WORKSHEET

1. What were the sales/revenues of the company for the last 12 months?

$ _____

2. What percent were they up for the last year?

_____ %

3. Adding the percent increase/decrease to the Trailing Twelve-Month Revenues, what are the **estimated sales/revenues** for the next 12 months?

$ _____

4. What is the average profit margin for this company?

_____ %

5. What is the industry average profit margin?

_____ %

6. Add the company's average profit margin to the industry average profit margin, and divide this figure by two—or in my terminology, calculate the **Estimated profit margin.**

_____ %

7. Multiply **estimated sales** by **estimated profit margin** to arrive at **Estimated profits.**

$ _____

8. How many shares does the company have outstanding?

_____

9. Divide estimated profits by total shares outstanding to arrive at **Estimated earnings per share.**

$ _____

10. Divide estimated earnings per share by the interest rate on a ten-year treasury to arrive at **Estimated Fair Market Value.**

$ _____

11. Is the Debt to Equity Ratio less than .20?

[ ] Yes   [ ] No

SECTION 1
SALES/REVENUES FOR THE LAST 12 MONTHS

You can find the company's sales/revenues for the last twelve months on many financial web sites or in the company's annual report.

Let's take a minute to define revenues and sales. Sales are what you get when you produce a product and sell it. Revenues are what you get for providing a service. Many companies both sell products and provide services for a fee. I'm constantly amazed that people invest in stocks and have never bothered to find out how much business the company is doing. You'll see on our worksheet that knowing how much in sales/revenues a business has is mandatory in being able to determine what a fair price for that company should be.

A business that has no sales, by the way, is not really a business in my book. It's a business *plan.* A lot of rookie investors get sucked into investing in companies that have never sold anything only to lose a substantial amount of money. It's not that you can't make money by investing in someone's dream—as a matter of fact, a lot of biotech companies got started that way—

it's just that the chances of you losing all of your money in a stock that doesn't have any sales or revenues are much, much higher than in a company that actually has customers. And remember, one of my goals is to get you to be able to identify a high return, *lower* risk idea.

Time to introduce you to our little friend (said in my best Al Pacino voice), ABC Company. ABC Company is a hypothetical company that I am going to use to illustrate how to fill out the worksheet as we go along. We looked up ABC Company's revenues for the last 12 months and found that ABC Company had $100 million in sales. Your worksheet should now look like the one on the next page.

ESTIMATED FAIR MARKET VALUE WORKSHEET

1. What were the sales/revenues of the company
for the last 12 months? $100 Million

2. What percent were they up for the last year? _____ %

3. Adding the percent increase/decrease to the
Trailing Twelve-Month Revenues, what are the
estimated sales/revenues for the next 12
months? $ _____

4. What is the average profit margin for this
company?   _____ %

5. What is the industry average profit margin?   _____ %

6. Add the company's average profit margin to
the industry average profit margin, and divide
this figure by two—or in my terminology,
calculate the **Estimated profit margin.**   _____ %

7. Multiply **estimated sales** by **estimated
profit margin** to arrive at **Estimated profits.** $ _____

8. How many shares does the company have
outstanding?   _____

9. Divide estimated profits by total shares
outstanding to arrive at **Estimated earnings
per share.** $ _____

10. Divide estimated earnings per share by the
interest rate on a ten-year treasury to arrive at
Estimated Fair Market Value. $ _____

11. Is the Debt to Equity Ratio less than .20?   [ ] Yes   [ ] No

SECTION 2
DETERMINING PERCENT OF SALES
INCREASE FOR THE LAST TWELVE MONTHS

Fortunately, you can also find this statistic on many free financial web sites. All you have to do is look it up and fill it in, or if you are doing the calculation by hand, simply take the difference of the last twelve months of revenues from the revenues for the year prior to that. Then divide that number by the prior year's revenues and move the decimal two places to the right.

For example, ABC Company is our hypothetical company that had $100 million in sales over the last twelve months. We found out by looking at their financial statements that the year prior to the last 12 months, ABC Company had $91 million in sales. Subtracting $91 million in revenues from the $100 million in revenues that ABC Company achieved over the last year tells us that sales improved by $9 million dollars. If we divide $9 million by $91 million, we get .099. Moving the decimal place to the right two places, we see that ABC Company's sales were up 9.9%. In future examples, I'm going to continue to use ABC Company, but I'm going to round up the increase in sales figure to 10% to keep the math simple.

On the next page, we've filled in line number 2 with the result. It should look like this . . .

ESTIMATED FAIR MARKET VALUE WORKSHEET

1. What were the sales/revenues of the company for the last 12 months? $100 Million

2. What percent were they up for the last year?   10%

3. Adding the percent increase/decrease to the Trailing Twelve-Month Revenues, what are the ***estimated sales/revenues*** for the next 12 months? $

4. What is the average profit margin for this company?   %

5. What is the industry average profit margin?   %

6. Add the company's average profit margin to the industry average profit margin, and divide this figure by two—or in my terminology, calculate the ***Estimated profit margin.***   %

7. Multiply ***estimated sales*** by ***estimated profit margin*** to arrive at ***Estimated profits.*** $

8. How many shares does the company have outstanding?

9. Divide estimated profits by total shares outstanding to arrive at ***Estimated earnings per share.*** $

10. Divide estimated earnings per share by the interest rate on a ten-year treasury to arrive at ***Estimated Fair Market Value.*** $

11. Is the Debt to Equity Ratio less than .20?   [ ] Yes   [ ] No

SECTION 3
ESTIMATING SALES FOR THE NEXT TWELVE MONTHS

To arrive at the estimated sales/ revenues, simply add the percentage increase over the past twelve months to the revenues for the past year, and write that on the third blank on our worksheet.

Let's go back to ABC Company. We know that ABC had $100 million in sales, up from $91 million the year before or roughly 10%. If ABC Company increases sales by 10% again over the next 12 months, then our **estimated sales/revenues** should come in at around $110 million.

By the way, if sales are growing by faster than 20%, I tend to add only 20% to the trailing 12 months sales figures. You can use your own judgment here. I don't like to project sales increases of much more than 20% year over year because experience has taught me that to increase sales by 20% per year consistently is a Herculean task. Very few companies have ever been capable of doing so for extended time periods, and personally, I'd rather make the error of being too conservative rather than too aggressive. But that's just me. If sales are increasing by 50% and you want to use that number as your estimate of future growth, just be aware of the fact that your **estimated fair market value** will be much higher. If the company fails to meet such high expectations, the results can be really negative. Wall Street language for a company that fails to meet sales or profit forecasts is "misses." And when a stock "misses," the next thing usually missing is much of the value the stock had the day before the report surfaced.

In addition, if sales are dropping by more than 10%, I will normally disregard the stock. Why? Because the long-term growth rate of the company is tied to its ability to grow its profits, and without sales growth, it becomes very difficult to grow profits. Make sense?

This may be a crude way of forecasting sales, but it's got its strong points. In fact, all you are doing is projecting the current trend for one year. And as to its accuracy, my method of forecasting sales tends to be at least as close as many of the analysts' projections that I've seen. As to the really long-term growth rate of the company, who knows? In this case, your guess is probably as good as mine—or anyone else's for that matter.

If you are having trouble accepting this method of forecasting sales, just keep this in mind. What you are really trying to do is to determine whether or not sales are rising (or at least not dropping significantly) and what you might be able to **reasonably** estimate. We are not trying to predict the exact sales number, which I'm pretty positive you couldn't do even if you were an expert in the field or even the CEO of the company. Remember, it is not necessary to be perfect in our projection to come up with a decent estimate. We are attempting to be profitable, not perfect.

Forecasting sales is one of the areas where most investors, professional and amateur alike, tend to get into big trouble. Professional analysts, being human, have a natural tendency to forecast unusually high rates of growth for businesses that they like. I've been to many a ***road show*** (a road show is a presentation the management of a company that is going public for the first time gives to many analysts and money managers across the country to generate interest in their stock) where the management has given compelling presentations that, I have to admit, are extremely impressive. These presentations are what I refer to as "***the story.***" The presentation may involve information regarding the expected growth of an industry, a new drug that will cure a disease, like cancer, the latest and greatest gadget that will revolutionize the way we travel or communicate, or something equally fantastic. All very interesting and exciting to someone who wants to make money investing in stocks.

As a young stockbroker, highly skilled presentations of "***the story***" were the main reason I had to develop a method of evaluating a stock that was independent of my emotions. Emotions and good investing generally do not mix well. If you've been investing for any length of time, you'll know exactly what I'm talking about. If you wonder what I'm talking about, don't worry, it'll become apparent over time.

Anyway, by focusing on the actual sales numbers I am concentrating on **facts**, not the "**story**." In other words, you are taking the first step to make sure that the company you are investigating has a sound financial foundation **before** you listen to **the story**.

One last note before we continue to the next section. When an industry is prone to swift and substantial change, it is incredibly difficult to forecast sales or revenues with any degree of accuracy. On the other hand, some industries tend to experience consistent demand for their product. Take the Technology and Food Industries for example. You don't **have** to buy the latest new cell phone, computer, software package, etc., but you *do* have to eat! In an economic pinch, also known as a recession, the decision between feeding your family or buying a new PC is an easy one (I hope). Therefore, food producers may be a little more predictable than technology manufacturers.

Stocks tied to commodity prices tend to be cyclical in nature and are difficult to forecast as well. Energy, Steel, and Auto Manufacturers come to mind here.

This is where common sense has to enter into investing. The more a service is **needed**, the higher its predictability and the easier it is to estimate sales.

Going back to the worksheet and filling in the numbers for ABC Company, it should now look like this . . .

ESTIMATED FAIR MARKET VALUE WORKSHEET

1. What were the sales/revenues of the company
for the last 12 months? $100 Million

2. What percent were they up for the last year?   10%

3. Adding the percent increase/decrease to the
Trailing Twelve-Month Revenues, what are the
estimated sales/revenues for the next 12
months? $110 Million

4. What is the average profit margin for this
company?   %

5. What is the industry average profit margin?   %

6. Add the company's average profit margin to
the industry average profit margin, and divide
this figure by two—or in my terminology,
calculate the *Estimated profit margin.*   %

7. Multiply *estimated sales* by *estimated
profit margin* to arrive at *Estimated profits.* $

8. How many shares does the company have
outstanding?

9. Divide estimated profits by total shares
outstanding to arrive at *Estimated earnings
per share.* $

10. Divide estimated earnings per share by the
interest rate on a ten-year treasury to arrive at
Estimated Fair Market Value. $

11. Is the Debt to Equity Ratio less than .20?   [ ] Yes   [ ] No

SECTIONS 4, 5, AND 6
ESTIMATING PROFIT MARGINS
(I cheated and combined these into one)

Many free financial web sites publish both the company's five-year average profit margin and the industry average profit margin. You can either use their information to fill in the worksheet, or you can estimate profit margins for the company and industry manually. Once you have both your company's five-year average profit margin and the industry average profit margin, simply add them together and divide by two to arrive at the estimated profit margin.

Before I get into the actual process of estimating profit margins, just let me say that estimating next year's profit margins makes estimating next year's sales look easy. There are so many things in a business that can change, both good and bad, that there is just no way to prepare for them all. That's why when I look at profit margins and am trying to make an **estimate**, I like to look at the company's historical profit margins over several years, as well as the average profit margins for the industry. Microsoft Money has already compiled the information on both the company's and the industry's average profit margins over the last five years. You can use those numbers if you wish—just remember what I said about inaccuracies earlier.

Value Line is the next easiest way to find this information. Value Line already has the company's profit margins calculated for each year. All you have to do is take an average of the profit margins for the company over the last five years. Then, look up the industry average profit margin. Add the two together and divide by two. If Value Line doesn't follow the stock or the industry that you are investigating, and you don't want to use the free information on Microsoft's web site, you're going to have to do this the hard way—by looking up the financial statements at the SEC's web site and calculating the numbers by hand.

If you are calculating the company's average profit margin by hand, you first have to calculate the profit margin (it's not prepared for you) by dividing the net income figure (accounting speak for profit) on the income statement by the sales/revenues. (You can find this information on the web at www.sec.gov.)

Let's assume you are doing the calculation by hand, and we are using ABC Company. We know that ABC Company had $100 million in revenues and $10 million in net income (profit) by looking at the income statement that we found on the SEC's web site. Dividing $10 million in profits by $100 million in sales gives us a 10% profit margin. Now do this for each of the last five years. When you're done, add the five years worth of profit margins together and divide by five. You now have the five-year average profit margin for ABC Company.

The reason I like to look back five years (or more if you have the data) is that over a five-year time period, a company will normally experience one business cycle, and you can get a good idea of what you should be able to expect in the future by seeing what happens in both good and bad times. In other words, you should get a good idea of the good, the bad, and the ugly. That way, you won't have a tendency to be overly optimistic, nor too pessimistic in your estimate. Again, our goal is not to be perfect but to make a *reasonable* estimate as to what is normal.

If you aren't going to use the free information available on the Internet or Value Line to look up the industry average profit margins, you should compute the five-year average profit margins for several of the company's competitors as well. Once you have determined the average profit margin for the company's competitors, take an average of all of these figures to arrive at an industry average profit margin yourself. Time consuming? You bet. Valuable? How many other people do you think will have had the determination to do what you just did? If you guessed not many, I'd say you were right. I'd be willing to bet that 95% of individual stockowners or their brokers have **never** done this. You can develop a tremendous edge on the investing public by performing such an exercise.

Anyway, this is probably a good time to go into the ***Bullington Reversion to the Mean Theory.***

The ***Bullington Reversion to the Mean Theory*** states that if there is an unusually large difference between ABC Company's

15

profit margin and the industry average profit margin, over time, the two average profit margins will move closer together.

An example may help here. Let's say ABC is twice as profitable as their competitors. You can bet that ABC's competitors are hard at work trying to find out how to duplicate whatever it is that ABC is doing in order to increase their own profit margins. Once they figure it out, you know what they'll do then? That's right, they'll go to ABC's customers and offer lower prices to try and lure away business. If they are successful, ABC will be forced to lower their own prices or may face losing customers. That's the nature of a competitive society. If you doubt what I'm saying, just ask Kmart if Wal-Mart was a threat. At one time, K-Mart was the dominate retailer of low cost goods in the country. Wal-Mart studied their processes and improved on them, enabling Wal-Mart to sell for even lower prices than K-Mart. Lower prices, lower profit margins (for K-mart anyway). Make sense?

On the other hand, if ABC had a profit margin that was less than the industry average, you can bet that the management of ABC is aware of the fact. Other groups that will be aware of that fact include the board of directors and the shareholders. You can bet that the management of ABC will be doing everything in its power to cut costs, boost revenues, and get in line with the industry averages. Why? Because if the management can't earn profit margins that are at least average, who needs them? In many cases, although not always, their jobs will be on the line!

So, in essence, the ***Bullington Reversion to the Mean Theory*** states that a good company with above average profits can experience lower profit margins once the competition has figured out how to duplicate their success. Conversely, the management of a company that is currently underperforming its peers will be under a lot of pressure to match the industry average profit margin, or they could face the possibility of losing their jobs. Therefore, whatever advantage or disadvantage the company is currently experiencing will eventually move more towards the average of the group.

As with anything in the stock market, this theory is not a hard and fast rule, hence the term theory. It is quite possible you will find companies that defy the theory completely due to a competitive edge that is defendable—or a sorry management team that is un-defendable.

In spite of that, I have found this method of estimating profit margins to be very useful. Later on in the book, I'll give you some examples on how to apply the formula in different scenarios.

I almost forgot the example for this section. We've found that ABC Company has averaged 10% profit margins for the last five years. It just so happens that the industry average is also 10%. Adding the two together and dividing by two gives us a 10% ***estimated profit margin.***

Filling in the blanks, your worksheet should now look like this . . .

ESTIMATED FAIR MARKET VALUE WORKSHEET

1. What were the sales/revenues of the company
for the last 12 months? $100 Million

2. What percent were they up for the last year?   10%

3. Adding the percent increase/decrease to the
Trailing Twelve-Month Revenues, what are the
estimated sales/revenues for the next 12
months? $110 Million

4. What is the average profit margin for this
company?   10%

5. What is the industry average profit margin?   10%

6. Add the company's average profit margin to
the industry average profit margin, and divide
this figure by two—or in my terminology,
calculate the ***Estimated profit margin.***   10%

7. Multiply ***estimated sales*** by ***estimated
profit margin*** to arrive at ***Estimated profits.*** $

8. How many shares does the company have
outstanding?   _____

9. Divide estimated profits by total shares
outstanding to arrive at ***Estimated earnings
per share.*** $

10. Divide estimated earnings per share by the
interest rate on a ten-year treasury to arrive at
Estimated Fair Market Value. $

11. Is the Debt to Equity Ratio less than .20?   [ ] Yes   [ ] No

SECTION 7
HOW TO CALCULATE ESTIMATED PROFITS

Multiply estimated sales by estimated profit margins.

Let's look at an example. We think that ABC Company will sell $110 million worth of items next year. We also believe that ABC Company will have somewhere around a 10% after-tax profit margin. Multiplying expected sales of $110 million by 10% gives us an $11 million estimated profit. I've filled that number in on the worksheet. Take a look.

ESTIMATED FAIR MARKET VALUE WORKSHEET

1. What were the sales/revenues of the company for the last 12 months? $100 Million

2. What percent were they up for the last year? 10%

3. Adding the percent increase/decrease to the Trailing Twelve-Month Revenues, what are the *estimated sales/revenues* for the next 12 months? $110 Million

4. What is the average profit margin for this company? 10%

5. What is the industry average profit margin? 10%

6. Add the company's average profit margin to the industry average profit margin, and divide this figure by two—or in my terminology, calculate the *Estimated profit margin.* 10%

7. Multiply *estimated sales* by *estimated profit margin* to arrive at *Estimated profits.* $11 Million

8. How many shares does the company have outstanding? _____

9. Divide estimated profits by total shares outstanding to arrive at *Estimated earnings per share.* $_____

10. Divide estimated earnings per share by the interest rate on a ten-year treasury to arrive at *Estimated Fair Market Value.* $_____

11. Is the Debt to Equity Ratio less than .20? [ ] Yes   [ ] No

SECTIONS 8 AND 9
HOW TO CALCULATE ESTIMATED
EARNINGS PER SHARE
(I'm cheating again)

Divide estimated profits by the number of shares outstanding.

You can find the total number of shares outstanding on many web sites, including Value Line. You may also find this information on the company's financial statements at the SEC's web site.

Taking our estimate of profits from the last section ($11 million), you simply divide that number by the total number of shares outstanding.

Going back to ABC Company, let's assume it has 11 million shares outstanding. If we divide our estimated profits of $11 million by 11 million shares outstanding, the Earnings Per Share, or EPS, would equal $1.

Earnings Per Share represent an **extremely significant concept** for you to understand. In **theory**, Earnings Per Share are the profits you'd receive for each share of stock you own, if the company paid out all profits as a cash dividend. Notice the emphasis on the word, ***theory.*** (In reality, if companies were forced to pay out all of their earnings as dividends, you'd see massive restatements of how much money companies were reporting as profits. Some would have good reasons but most would not.) Profits are what people go into business for. It's why they invest. The EPS is the measure of how profitable a company has been on a per share basis. Nothing more, nothing less. By estimating the EPS yourself, you are really close to being able to tell what the stock should sell for under normal conditions. That is coming up in the next section.

Before we continue, I'd like to point out that many analysts publish estimates of earnings per share, or EPS. It would be really easy and less time consuming to use the analysts' estimate and skip all of the work that we've just done.

However, we are being responsible investors by trying to make sure there is nothing out of the ordinary with the estimate. Remember the "***story***" and that analysts are people, too. They can and will be influenced from time to time by great stories with little else backing them up (for more than one reason we won't get into).

I promise you, Warren Buffet doesn't rely on analyst estimates when he's getting ready to buy a company. And if Warren Buffet, one of the richest men in the world who can afford lots of mistakes, is not willing to take an analyst's word for it, why should you? It's not that you should never consider an analyst's word—I read analysts' reports all the time, and then I check the numbers out for myself. The saying, "Trust but verify" comes to mind here.

In a nutshell, if I were forced to give just one piece of advice to an individual that wanted to pick stocks, it would be, *"DO YOUR OWN WORK!"*

Or find someone to work with that **you know** will do his or her own work. As a matter of fact, this guide would probably be the best gift you could give your broker/financial advisor.

Unfortunately for the investing public, and the careers of many financial advisors, there is an unusually large likelihood that they are unfamiliar with the basic concepts we have just covered. I'd be willing to guess that roughly 90% of the individual investors and their advisors tend to take shortcuts by not performing these exercises, which in many cases will lead them to be just another carcass on the side of the stock market highway.

By the way, how do you know your advisor has done the work? Very simple—just ask him the questions on the worksheet about companies that you own or the companies they are recommending. If he/she doesn't know the answers, and you happen to like the financial advisor, send them a copy of this book. If they get it, read it, and still don't know the answers when you are discussing your stocks, you may want to find another advisor.

There I go, digressing again. Anyway, your worksheet should now look like this . . .

ESTIMATED FAIR MARKET VALUE WORKSHEET

1. What were the sales/revenues of the company
for the last 12 months? $100 Million

2. What percent were they up for the last year?   10%

3. Adding the percent increase/decrease to the
Trailing Twelve-Month Revenues, what are the
estimated sales/revenues for the next 12
months? $110 Million

4. What is the average profit margin for this
company?   10%

5. What is the industry average profit margin?   10%

6. Add the company's average profit margin to
the industry average profit margin, and divide
this figure by two—or in my terminology,
calculate the ***Estimated profit margin.***   10%

7. Multiply ***estimated sales*** by ***estimated
profit margin*** to arrive at ***Estimated profits.*** $11 Million

8. How many shares does the company have
outstanding?   11 Million

9. Divide estimated profits by total shares
outstanding to arrive at ***Estimated earnings
per share.*** $1.00

10. Divide estimated earnings per share by the
interest rate on a ten-year treasury to arrive at
Estimated Fair Market Value. $

11. Is the Debt to Equity Ratio less than .20?   [ ] Yes   [ ] No

SECTION 10
ESTIMATING FAIR MARKET VALUE

Divide the estimated earnings per share by the current interest rate on the ten-year treasury.

In the long run, interest rates on ten-year treasuries average between 5–6% per year. I tend to use 5% as a minimum when I make my own calculation on **estimated fair market value**. You can use the current rate if you'd like, which is significantly below average. The basic concept here is that the ten-year treasury has **averaged** a rate of return of roughly 5%–6%* per year over the last several decades, and I'd never settle for something that looks as though it's going to return **less than** the average return on the ten-year treasury. Does that make sense?

*If the rate on the ten-year treasury gets significantly higher than 5 or 6%, I will use that new number in future calculations. It will have the impact of reducing the estimated fair market value significantly.

Let's take a look at our worksheet before continuing . . .

ESTIMATED FAIR MARKET VALUE WORKSHEET

1. What were the sales/revenues of the company for the last 12 months? $100 Million

2. What percent were they up for the last year?   10%

3. Adding the percent increase/decrease to the Trailing Twelve-Month Revenues, what are the **estimated sales/revenues** for the next 12 months? $110 Million

4. What is the average profit margin for this company?   10%

5. What is the industry average profit margin?   10%

6. Add the company's average profit margin to the industry average profit margin, and divide this figure by two—or in my terminology, calculate the **Estimated profit margin.**   10%

7. Multiply **estimated sales** by **estimated profit margin** to arrive at **Estimated profits.** $11 Million

8. How many shares does the company have outstanding?   11 Million

9. Divide estimated profits by total shares outstanding to arrive at **Estimated earnings per share.** $1.00

10. Divide estimated earnings per share by the interest rate on a ten-year treasury to arrive at **Estimated Fair Market Value.** $20.00

11. Is the Debt to Equity Ratio less than .20?   [ ] Yes   [ ] No

In other words, if I owned every share of ABC Company and paid $20 dollars per share for it, my profits per share of $1 would equal 5% of my purchase price. **If I owned a company and paid more than $20 per share for a stock, with $1 per share in profits, I'd be getting a return of less than 5% on my money, and to me that is totally unacceptable.** Why would I want to earn *less* than the average rate of return of a government bond?

On the other hand, if a company I estimate can earn $1 per share, and I was able to purchase its stock for $10 or $15, I might really be interested. Make sense?

SECTION 11
THE DEBT TO EQUITY RATIO

You can look up the Debt to Equity Ratio on a number of financial web sites. To calculate this number manually, divide the total debt by shareholder's equity The number you arrive at should be less than .20. In other words, the debt is less than 20% of the company's assets as they appear on the balance sheet.

Let's assume you have investigated a company, filled out your worksheet, and the stock seems to be under priced. Sales are growing, and it has a good story. There is one last item to check out before you make your investment. That item is how to deal with companies that have debt. By analyzing the debt to equity ratio and making sure the debt is substantially lower than the assets a company has, or at least is showing on their balance sheet, you are reducing the risk of losing all of your money in the case of a bankruptcy. Notice I didn't say you were eliminating the risk, just reducing it. Again, our goal is to be able to identify lower risk, high return ideas.

There are certain industries where it is normal to have high debt to equity ratios. As a beginner, you'd be better off avoiding these situations and the higher risk that accompanies them.

Now your worksheet should look like this . . .

ESTIMATED FAIR MARKET VALUE WORKSHEET

1. What were the sales/revenues of the company for the last 12 months? $100 Million

2. What percent were they up for the last year?   10%

3. Adding the percent increase/decrease to the Trailing Twelve-Month Revenues, what are the ***estimated sales/revenues*** for the next 12 months? $110 Million

4. What is the average profit margin for this company?   10%

5. What is the industry average profit margin?   10%

6. Add the company's average profit margin to the industry average profit margin, and divide this figure by two—or in my terminology, calculate the ***Estimated profit margin.***   10%

7. Multiply ***estimated sales*** by ***estimated profit margin*** to arrive at ***Estimated profits.*** $11 Million

8. How many shares does the company have outstanding?   11 Million

9. Divide estimated profits by total shares outstanding to arrive at ***Estimated earnings per share.*** $1.00

10. Divide estimated earnings per share by the interest rate on a ten-year treasury to arrive at ***Estimated Fair Market Value.*** $20.00

11. Is the Debt to Equity Ratio less than .20?   [✓] Yes [ ] No

GUIDELINES

In closing the book, I'd like to offer some advice in constructing a portfolio of stocks. I'd also like to share with you some knowledge on how stock prices actually move. A really good exercise I would highly recommend is to go back and do these calculations on past data. You can get an old copy of Value Line to gather the old sales and profit margin figures you will need. If you don't have a subscription, go to a library, copy some pages, take them home, and fill out some worksheets on these companies. What you will find is that some companies can stray extremely far away from the estimated fair market value, sometimes for years!

This is actually what happened in the stock market of 1995–2000. Many really good companies were selling for 4–5 times, some even 10 times, my estimated fair market value. Their stocks reached prices that should have taken them years to grow into at very high growth rates. In some cases, companies would have needed to grow at 40% or better for at least ten years to reach the levels of sales and profit margins that these companies would have needed to do in order to justify the prices their stocks were selling for!

The fact that a company's stock price can stray far away from its estimated fair market value and remain extended, sometimes for years, is not limited to overpriced stocks either. Many stocks can and do remain undervalued for long time periods as well. If you do the recommended exercise and look at past performance, you will see exactly what I'm talking about. You'll find companies that sold at prices that were so low relative to the fair market price you'll come up with using the worksheet that you'll have to wonder what investors were thinking that caused them to become so pessimistic—and stay so pessimistic for so long.

The fact that stocks tend to move so far away from a normal price and then take what seems to be an incredibly long time to get back to that level is without a doubt the number one reason that investing in stocks is so difficult. Your success is going to be dependent on your having the tenacity to do the work and then giving the stock enough time to move the way you thought it should.

Having said that, let's get specific with recommendations. I would generally recommend that you look for stocks selling below the estimated fair market value. I prefer to invest in stocks that are selling for about half that number. I feel that by investing in companies that are selling at prices that are much lower than they should be, and that have very little debt, the potential gain is greater and the potential risk is somewhat lower. The idea is that by investing in stocks that are selling below where they should be, you will invariably take less risk than by investing in a great company with a great product selling at 4 or 5 times the *estimated fair market value*. Make sense?

On top of that, I'd like to point out that good companies that are not selling below fair market value might make good long-term investments; it's just that you shouldn't expect miracles right away. If you get lucky and make money immediately, then great! It does happen from time to time.

Good stocks to investigate are all around you. Good stock ideas (in addition to investigating tips from friends) can be found in *Fortune* magazine, *Baron's*, and *The Wall Street Journal*. There are many other excellent financial publications as well. Just remember to complete a worksheet *before you invest*. You could scan the list of stocks making new 52-week lows found in many newspapers and do some worksheets on the companies appearing there. Before you panic thinking of all of the work involved, let me remind you that once you've had some practice filling out the worksheet, it probably won't take you more than a couple of minutes to fill one out.

When I'll Sell a Stock

I'll generally hold a stock until it reaches my estimated fair market value or until the sales/revenues begin to drop by more than 10%. In some cases, I'll sell a stock because I've found another one that I like better than the ones I'm holding now. Many stocks will continue to keep rising after a stock reaches its estimated fair market value, as investors tend to get excited by the rapid price movement. If I really like the company, I'll sell half at its estimated fair market value and utilize another method of selling that is based on price movement to try and capture some of the additional gains. I don't want to overload you with that information now, but as I mentioned earlier, I'll be writing about those techniques in another book.

PUTTING IT ALL TOGETHER
"HOW MUCH DIVERSIFICATION IS ENOUGH?"

This is easier than all of the other material combined. The ideal portfolio, in my opinion, is between 15 to 20 stocks, assuming you've been able to locate that many stocks that pass the worksheet test. By the way, if you can't find stocks that meet all of the criteria—selling below market value, a good story, low debt, etc.—then leave the money in cash. You're going to have to trust me on this one. You will be better off in the long run saving your portfolio for only the types of stocks that you really want to own. Sticking to the rule of only holding 15 to 20 stock means that you won't commit more than 4–5% of your *stock* portfolio to any one position (and very few people can afford the risk of being 100% invested in stocks).

Anyway, a lot of people get really frustrated when I tell them to limit their investments to 4 or 5% of their stock portfolio because they'd really like to put all of their money into one stock and shoot for the moon. These people are concentrating on the returns without thinking about the risk. This is generally not a good idea. A better idea is to concentrate on how much better risk control you have than an average mutual fund does and how you can best take advantage of that by not being forced to invest in anything that doesn't meet all of your criteria.

Think about this for a second. Most stock mutual funds don't have the luxury of holding large amounts of cash. They have to stay invested because their prospectus says so. Even if the manager hates market conditions and can't find stocks that he or she feels are compelling investments, they have to remain invested. You can remain comfortably in cash for as long as necessary until you find stocks that meet the criteria you are looking for. There are many advantages to being your own portfolio manager. In my opinion, the ability to remain heavily invested in cash is one of the biggest.

Also, did you know that most stock mutual funds are prevented from owning controlling interests in a company? A controlling interest is defined as more than 7% of that company's stock. If you are a large mutual fund, you may have to limit your investment to less than 1% of your fund's assets to comply with this rule. So now, if the stock doubles, you will earn less than 1% for your fund. As a matter of fact, the average position a mutual fund portfolio will hold in one particular stock is typically around 1–2% of the fund's assets. If this stock goes up by 100–200%, they've earned 1 or 2% for their fund. Woo hoo! (That's a totally sarcastic woo hoo, by the way).

On the other hand, if you the individual investor have a 5% position in that same stock, when it doubles, you've earned 5–10% on your entire portfolio even if all of your other money remained in cash! When you hit on a stock that goes up several hundred percent, you might increase your whole portfolio value by 20% or more! When you invest in three or four stocks that do that in unison, you double the value of your stock portfolio in one year! Can't wait for those days to return, can you? Me either.

The last paragraph illustrates another advantage the individual investor has—the ability to concentrate his or her investments in companies with above average return potential and below average risk. Every portfolio manager in the country would love to have the same advantages you have.

In Conclusion

So that's it. I hear a story and immediately check out the numbers by doing the worksheet. If I find that the stock is undervalued and I like the story, and they meet the debt criteria, I make an investment of as much as 4 or 5% of my stock portfolio value. I keep buying stocks for my portfolio until the stock portion of my portfolio is fully invested or until I can't find any stocks that I feel merit an investment, in which case, I'll keep looking. Sooner or later, something is bound to turn up.

I'll generally sell at least half of my stock when it's reached fair market value, when I find a better stock, or when the sales and profits drop by more than 10%.

I'm almost embarrassed at how simple the whole process really is. I feel like I have to warn you though—simple isn't the same thing as easy. Dieting is simple, but it isn't easy. Investing the right way is right up there in level of difficulty with dieting. I like to think of investing as the ultimate microcosm of life. You will experience just about every emotion imaginable, and it's very rarely boring. Done well, over long time periods, you can build a substantial net worth, have fun, pull your hair out, fantasize . . . well, you get the picture.

Feel free to write or call with your opinions on this book. You can go to my firm's web site at BullingtonCapital.com to get in touch with me.

Good luck, and good stock picking!